50 New Orleans Recipes for Home

By: Kelly Johnson

Table of Contents

- Shrimp Étouffée
- Jambalaya
- Crawfish Boil
- Red Beans and Rice
- Beignets
- Gumbo
- Muffuletta Sandwich
- Po' Boy Sandwich (Shrimp, Oyster, or Catfish)
- Bananas Foster
- King Cake
- Oysters Rockefeller
- Shrimp Creole
- Andouille Sausage
- Bread Pudding with Whiskey Sauce
- Turtle Soup
- Fried Alligator Bites
- Crab Cakes
- Dirty Rice
- Cajun Fried Chicken
- Maque Choux (Corn and Peppers)
- Pralines
- Cajun Shrimp Pasta
- Cajun Shrimp and Grits
- Catfish Courtbouillon
- Blackened Fish (Redfish or Catfish)
- Cajun Crab Dip
- Creole Tomato Salad
- Cajun Cornbread
- Bourbon Street Chicken
- Mirliton Casserole
- Seafood Gumbo
- Cajun Shrimp Etouffee
- Redfish Courtbouillon
- Chicken and Sausage Gumbo
- Cajun Crawfish Pie
- Cajun Shrimp and Crab Boil

- New Orleans BBQ Shrimp
- Cajun Corn Maque Choux
- Stuffed Bell Peppers (Cajun Style)
- Cajun Red Beans and Rice
- Cajun Chicken and Sausage Jambalaya
- Cajun Boudin Balls
- Cajun Dirty Rice
- Cajun Blackened Catfish
- Shrimp Po' Boy with Remoulade Sauce
- Cajun Crab Cakes with Creole Mustard Sauce
- Cajun Shrimp and Andouille Sausage Pasta
- Cajun Shrimp and Crab Salad
- Cajun Chicken and Sausage Gumbo
- Cajun Shrimp and Sausage Jambalaya

Shrimp Étouffée

Ingredients:

- 1/2 cup unsalted butter
- 1/2 cup all-purpose flour
- 1 large onion, finely chopped
- 1 green bell pepper, finely chopped
- 2 celery stalks, finely chopped
- 4 cloves garlic, minced
- 1 cup diced tomatoes
- 2 cups seafood or chicken broth
- 1/2 cup chopped green onions
- 1/4 cup chopped fresh parsley
- 1 teaspoon paprika
- 1/2 teaspoon cayenne pepper (adjust to taste)
- 1/2 teaspoon dried thyme
- Salt and black pepper to taste
- 1 lb (450g) large shrimp, peeled and deveined
- Cooked white rice, for serving

Instructions:

1. In a large skillet or Dutch oven, melt the butter over medium heat. Gradually add the flour, stirring constantly to make a roux. Cook the roux, stirring frequently, until it turns a dark caramel color, about 20-25 minutes. Be careful not to burn it.
2. Add the chopped onion, bell pepper, celery, and garlic to the skillet. Cook, stirring occasionally, until the vegetables are softened, about 5-7 minutes.
3. Stir in the diced tomatoes and cook for another 2-3 minutes.
4. Gradually pour in the seafood or chicken broth, stirring constantly to prevent lumps from forming. Bring the mixture to a simmer.
5. Add the chopped green onions, parsley, paprika, cayenne pepper, dried thyme, salt, and black pepper to the skillet. Stir well to combine.
6. Reduce the heat to low and simmer the mixture for 15-20 minutes, stirring occasionally, to allow the flavors to meld together and the sauce to thicken.
7. Add the peeled and deveined shrimp to the skillet. Cook for 5-7 minutes, or until the shrimp are pink and cooked through.

8. Taste and adjust the seasoning with more salt, pepper, or cayenne pepper if needed.
9. Serve the shrimp étouffée hot over cooked white rice.

Garnish with additional chopped green onions and parsley if desired.

10. Enjoy your delicious Shrimp Étouffée, a classic New Orleans dish!

Jambalaya

Ingredients:

- 1 lb (450g) boneless, skinless chicken thighs, diced
- 1 lb (450g) Andouille sausage, sliced into rounds
- 1 large onion, chopped
- 1 green bell pepper, chopped
- 2 celery stalks, chopped
- 4 cloves garlic, minced
- 1 can (14.5 oz) diced tomatoes, undrained
- 3 cups chicken broth
- 1 1/2 cups long-grain white rice
- 1 tablespoon Cajun seasoning
- 1 teaspoon dried thyme
- 1 teaspoon dried oregano
- 1/2 teaspoon paprika
- 1/2 teaspoon cayenne pepper (adjust to taste)
- Salt and black pepper to taste
- 1 lb (450g) large shrimp, peeled and deveined
- Chopped green onions, for garnish
- Chopped fresh parsley, for garnish

Instructions:

1. In a large Dutch oven or heavy-bottomed pot, heat some oil over medium-high heat. Add the diced chicken thighs and Andouille sausage slices. Cook until browned, about 5-7 minutes. Remove the chicken and sausage from the pot and set aside.
2. In the same pot, add a bit more oil if needed. Add the chopped onion, bell pepper, and celery. Cook, stirring occasionally, until the vegetables are softened, about 5 minutes. Add the minced garlic and cook for an additional minute.
3. Stir in the diced tomatoes (with their juices), chicken broth, rice, Cajun seasoning, dried thyme, dried oregano, paprika, cayenne pepper, salt, and black pepper. Bring the mixture to a boil.
4. Reduce the heat to low, cover, and simmer for about 20 minutes, or until the rice is almost tender and most of the liquid is absorbed.
5. Stir in the cooked chicken and sausage back into the pot. Add the peeled and deveined shrimp. Cover and cook for another 5-7 minutes, or until the shrimp are pink and cooked through.
6. Taste and adjust the seasoning with more salt, pepper, or Cajun seasoning if needed.

Serve the Jambalaya hot, garnished with chopped green onions and fresh parsley.

7. Enjoy your delicious and flavorful Jambalaya!

Crawfish Boil

Ingredients:

- 5 lbs (2.25 kg) live crawfish
- 5 gallons (about 19 liters) water
- 2 cups (480 ml) liquid crab boil seasoning
- 2 cups (480 ml) kosher salt
- 2 cups (480 ml) Cajun seasoning
- 10-12 small red potatoes, halved
- 4 ears of corn, husked and halved
- 2 lbs (900g) smoked sausage, cut into 2-inch pieces
- 4 lemons, halved
- Hot sauce, for serving
- Melted butter, for serving
- Cocktail sauce, for serving

Instructions:

1. Fill a large stockpot with 5 gallons of water and place it over high heat on an outdoor propane burner.
2. Add the liquid crab boil seasoning, kosher salt, and Cajun seasoning to the water. Stir well to combine.
3. Once the water comes to a rolling boil, add the halved red potatoes to the pot. Cook for about 10-15 minutes, or until the potatoes are just starting to become tender.
4. Add the halved ears of corn and smoked sausage pieces to the pot. Continue to boil for another 5 minutes.
5. Carefully add the live crawfish to the boiling water. Stir gently to ensure that all the crawfish are submerged.
6. Bring the water back to a boil and cook the crawfish for about 5-7 minutes. They will turn bright red and float to the top when they are cooked.
7. Turn off the heat and let the crawfish soak in the seasoned water for about 15-20 minutes. This allows them to absorb more flavor.
8. Using a large strainer or crawfish basket, lift the crawfish, potatoes, corn, and sausage out of the pot and transfer them to a large serving platter or a table covered with newspaper.

9. Squeeze the lemon halves over the boiled crawfish and vegetables.
10. Serve the crawfish boil hot with hot sauce, melted butter, and cocktail sauce on the side.
11. Provide plenty of napkins and enjoy the messy, delicious feast with friends and family!

Note: Remember to discard any crawfish that are dead before cooking and rinse them thoroughly under cold water before adding them to the boiling pot. Also, be sure to have plenty of paper towels or napkins on hand, as eating crawfish can be messy!

Red Beans and Rice

Ingredients:

- 1 lb (450g) dried red kidney beans
- 1 lb (450g) smoked sausage or Andouille sausage, sliced into rounds
- 1 large onion, chopped
- 1 green bell pepper, chopped
- 2 celery stalks, chopped
- 4 cloves garlic, minced
- 6 cups (1.4 liters) chicken broth or water
- 2 bay leaves
- 1 teaspoon dried thyme
- 1 teaspoon dried oregano
- 1/2 teaspoon cayenne pepper (adjust to taste)
- Salt and black pepper to taste
- Cooked white rice, for serving
- Chopped green onions, for garnish
- Hot sauce, for serving

Instructions:

1. Rinse the dried red kidney beans under cold water and remove any debris. Place the beans in a large bowl and cover them with water. Let them soak overnight, or for at least 8 hours. Drain and rinse the beans before cooking.
2. In a large Dutch oven or heavy-bottomed pot, heat some oil over medium-high heat. Add the sliced sausage rounds and cook until browned, about 5-7 minutes. Remove the sausage from the pot and set aside.
3. In the same pot, add a bit more oil if needed. Add the chopped onion, bell pepper, and celery. Cook, stirring occasionally, until the vegetables are softened, about 5 minutes. Add the minced garlic and cook for an additional minute.
4. Return the cooked sausage to the pot. Add the soaked and drained red kidney beans, chicken broth or water, bay leaves, dried thyme, dried oregano, cayenne pepper, salt, and black pepper. Stir well to combine.
5. Bring the mixture to a boil, then reduce the heat to low. Cover and simmer for about 1 1/2 to 2 hours, or until the beans are tender and creamy, stirring occasionally. If the mixture becomes too thick, you can add more broth or water as needed.
6. Once the beans are cooked, taste and adjust the seasoning with more salt, pepper, or cayenne pepper if needed.
7. Serve the Red Beans and Rice hot over cooked white rice.
8. Garnish with chopped green onions and serve with hot sauce on the side.

9. Enjoy your flavorful and comforting Red Beans and Rice, a quintessential New Orleans dish!

Beignets

Ingredients:

- 1 cup (240 ml) lukewarm water
- 2 1/4 teaspoons (1 packet) active dry yeast
- 1/4 cup (50g) granulated sugar
- 2 large eggs
- 1 teaspoon vanilla extract
- 1 cup (240 ml) evaporated milk
- 4 cups (500g) all-purpose flour, plus more for dusting
- 1/4 cup (55g) unsalted butter, melted
- 1/2 teaspoon salt
- Vegetable oil, for frying
- Powdered sugar, for dusting

Instructions:

1. In a small bowl, combine the lukewarm water and active dry yeast. Let it sit for about 5 minutes until the yeast is dissolved and becomes frothy.
2. In a large mixing bowl or the bowl of a stand mixer, combine the yeast mixture, granulated sugar, eggs, vanilla extract, and evaporated milk. Mix well.
3. Gradually add the flour to the wet ingredients, mixing until a soft dough forms.
4. Add the melted butter and salt to the dough, and continue to mix until well combined.
5. If using a stand mixer, knead the dough with the dough hook attachment for about 5-7 minutes until it is smooth and elastic. If kneading by hand, turn the dough out onto a floured surface and knead for about 10 minutes.
6. Place the dough in a greased bowl, cover with a clean kitchen towel or plastic wrap, and let it rise in a warm place for about 1-2 hours, or until doubled in size.
7. Once the dough has risen, punch it down and turn it out onto a floured surface. Roll the dough out to about 1/4-inch thickness.
8. Using a sharp knife or pizza cutter, cut the dough into squares or rectangles, about 2-3 inches in size.
9. Heat vegetable oil in a deep fryer or large pot to 350°F (175°C).
10. Carefully add the beignet squares to the hot oil in batches, frying them for about 2-3 minutes on each side, or until they are golden brown and puffed up.
11. Remove the fried beignets from the oil using a slotted spoon or spider strainer, and drain them on paper towels to remove excess oil.
12. Repeat the frying process with the remaining dough squares.
13. Once all the beignets are fried, dust them generously with powdered sugar while they are still warm.
14. Serve the beignets immediately, and enjoy them with a cup of coffee or hot chocolate.

15. Bon appétit!

Gumbo

Ingredients:

- 1/2 cup (120 ml) vegetable oil
- 1/2 cup (65g) all-purpose flour
- 1 large onion, chopped
- 1 green bell pepper, chopped
- 2 celery stalks, chopped
- 4 cloves garlic, minced
- 1 lb (450g) Andouille sausage, sliced into rounds
- 1 lb (450g) boneless, skinless chicken thighs, diced
- 6 cups (1.4 liters) chicken broth
- 1 can (14.5 oz) diced tomatoes, undrained
- 2 bay leaves
- 1 teaspoon dried thyme
- 1 teaspoon dried oregano
- 1/2 teaspoon cayenne pepper (adjust to taste)
- Salt and black pepper to taste
- 1 lb (450g) large shrimp, peeled and deveined
- 1 lb (450g) okra, sliced (fresh or frozen)
- Cooked white rice, for serving
- Chopped green onions, for garnish

Instructions:

1. In a large Dutch oven or heavy-bottomed pot, heat the vegetable oil over medium heat. Gradually add the flour, stirring constantly to make a roux. Cook the roux, stirring frequently, until it turns a dark caramel color, about 20-25 minutes. Be careful not to burn it.
2. Add the chopped onion, bell pepper, celery, and minced garlic to the pot. Cook, stirring occasionally, until the vegetables are softened, about 5-7 minutes.
3. Add the sliced Andouille sausage and diced chicken thighs to the pot. Cook, stirring occasionally, until the chicken is browned on all sides, about 5-7 minutes.
4. Gradually pour in the chicken broth, stirring constantly to prevent lumps from forming. Add the diced tomatoes (with their juices), bay leaves, dried thyme, dried oregano, cayenne pepper, salt, and black pepper. Stir well to combine.
5. Bring the mixture to a simmer, then reduce the heat to low. Cover and let the gumbo simmer for about 1 hour, stirring occasionally.
6. After 1 hour, add the peeled and deveined shrimp and sliced okra to the pot. Continue to simmer the gumbo for another 10-15 minutes, or until the shrimp are pink and cooked through.

7. Taste and adjust the seasoning with more salt, pepper, or cayenne pepper if needed.
8. Remove the bay leaves from the pot before serving.
9. Serve the gumbo hot over cooked white rice.
10. Garnish each serving with chopped green onions.
11. Enjoy your delicious and hearty New Orleans Gumbo!

Muffuletta Sandwich

Ingredients:

- 1 round loaf of Italian bread (about 10 inches in diameter)
- 1/2 cup olive salad (see recipe below)
- 4 ounces (115g) sliced Genoa salami
- 4 ounces (115g) sliced ham
- 4 ounces (115g) sliced mortadella
- 4 ounces (115g) sliced provolone cheese
- 4 ounces (115g) sliced mozzarella cheese

For the Olive Salad:

- 1 cup pitted green olives, chopped
- 1 cup pitted black olives, chopped
- 1/2 cup roasted red bell peppers, chopped
- 2 cloves garlic, minced
- 1/4 cup chopped fresh parsley
- 2 tablespoons capers, chopped
- 1/4 cup olive oil
- 2 tablespoons red wine vinegar
- 1 teaspoon dried oregano
- Salt and black pepper to taste

Instructions:

1. To make the olive salad, combine the chopped green olives, black olives, roasted red bell peppers, minced garlic, chopped parsley, chopped capers, olive oil, red wine vinegar, dried oregano, salt, and black pepper in a bowl. Mix well to combine. Cover and refrigerate for at least 1 hour to allow the flavors to meld together.
2. Slice the round loaf of Italian bread horizontally to create a top and bottom half. Hollow out some of the bread from the inside of both halves to create space for the fillings.
3. Spread a generous layer of olive salad on the bottom half of the bread.
4. Layer the sliced Genoa salami, ham, mortadella, provolone cheese, and mozzarella cheese on top of the olive salad.

5. Place the top half of the bread on top of the fillings and press down gently to compress the sandwich.
6. Wrap the Muffuletta sandwich tightly in plastic wrap or foil and refrigerate for at least 1 hour, or overnight, to allow the flavors to meld together and the sandwich to set.
7. When ready to serve, unwrap the sandwich and use a serrated knife to cut it into wedges.
8. Serve the Muffuletta wedges cold or at room temperature.
9. Enjoy your delicious and flavorful Muffuletta Sandwich, a classic New Orleans favorite!

Po' Boy Sandwich (Shrimp, Oyster, or Catfish)

Ingredients:

For the Remoulade Sauce:

- 1/2 cup mayonnaise
- 2 tablespoons Creole or whole-grain mustard
- 1 tablespoon prepared horseradish
- 1 tablespoon lemon juice
- 1 teaspoon Worcestershire sauce
- 1 clove garlic, minced
- 1/2 teaspoon paprika
- 1/2 teaspoon hot sauce (adjust to taste)
- Salt and black pepper to taste

For the Sandwich:

- 1 lb (450g) shrimp, oysters, or catfish fillets
- 1 cup buttermilk
- 1 cup all-purpose flour
- 1/2 cup cornmeal
- 1/2 teaspoon salt
- 1/2 teaspoon black pepper
- Vegetable oil, for frying
- French bread or baguette, cut into sandwich-sized pieces
- Shredded lettuce
- Sliced tomatoes
- Sliced pickles
- Sliced onions (optional)
- Remoulade sauce (see recipe above)

Instructions:

1. To make the Remoulade Sauce, whisk together the mayonnaise, mustard, horseradish, lemon juice, Worcestershire sauce, minced garlic, paprika, hot sauce, salt, and black pepper in a bowl. Cover and refrigerate until ready to use.
2. If using shrimp, peel and devein them. If using oysters or catfish fillets, rinse them and pat dry with paper towels.

3. Place the seafood (shrimp, oysters, or catfish) in a bowl and pour the buttermilk over them. Let them soak in the buttermilk for about 15-20 minutes.
4. In a shallow dish, combine the all-purpose flour, cornmeal, salt, and black pepper.
5. Heat vegetable oil in a large skillet or deep fryer to 350°F (175°C).
6. Remove the seafood from the buttermilk, allowing any excess to drip off. Dredge the seafood in the flour mixture, shaking off any excess.
7. Carefully place the seafood in the hot oil and fry until golden brown and crispy, about 2-3 minutes per side. Depending on the size of your skillet or fryer, you may need to fry the seafood in batches.
8. Remove the fried seafood from the oil and drain on paper towels to remove excess oil.
9. To assemble the Po' Boy sandwiches, spread a generous amount of Remoulade sauce on the cut sides of the French bread or baguette.
10. Arrange shredded lettuce, sliced tomatoes, sliced pickles, and sliced onions (if using) on one side of the bread.
11. Place the fried seafood on top of the vegetables.
12. Close the sandwich with the other half of the bread.
13. Serve the Po' Boy sandwiches immediately, and enjoy the crispy, flavorful goodness!
14. Serve with additional Remoulade sauce on the side for dipping, if desired.

Bananas Foster

Ingredients:

- 4 ripe bananas, peeled and sliced
- 1/4 cup (55g) unsalted butter
- 1/2 cup (100g) packed brown sugar
- 1/4 teaspoon ground cinnamon
- 1/4 cup (60 ml) dark rum
- 1/4 cup (60 ml) banana liqueur (optional)
- Vanilla ice cream, for serving

Instructions:

1. In a large skillet or sauté pan, melt the butter over medium heat.
2. Add the brown sugar and ground cinnamon to the skillet, stirring until the sugar is dissolved and the mixture is smooth.
3. Add the sliced bananas to the skillet, tossing gently to coat them in the butter-sugar mixture. Cook for about 2-3 minutes, or until the bananas are slightly softened.
4. Carefully add the dark rum to the skillet. If using banana liqueur, add it as well. Be cautious as the alcohol may ignite when added to the hot pan. If desired, you can ignite the mixture with a long lighter or match, but be sure to do so carefully and keep a lid nearby to smother the flames if necessary.
5. Allow the mixture to simmer for another 2-3 minutes, stirring gently, until the sauce has thickened slightly and the alcohol has cooked off.
6. Remove the skillet from the heat.
7. Serve the Bananas Foster immediately over scoops of vanilla ice cream.
8. Drizzle any remaining sauce from the skillet over the top of the ice cream.
9. Enjoy your decadent and delicious Bananas Foster dessert!

Note: Be cautious when working with alcohol and open flames. If you're uncomfortable with flaming the dish, you can skip that step and simply allow the alcohol to cook off on the stovetop. The dish will still be delicious!

King Cake

Ingredients:

For the Dough:

- 1 cup warm milk (110°F/45°C)
- 2 packages (14g) active dry yeast
- 1/2 cup granulated sugar
- 1/2 cup (1 stick) unsalted butter, melted
- 2 large eggs
- 1 teaspoon vanilla extract
- 1 teaspoon salt
- 1/2 teaspoon ground nutmeg
- 1/2 teaspoon ground cinnamon
- 4 1/2 cups all-purpose flour

For the Filling:

- 1/2 cup packed brown sugar
- 1/2 cup granulated sugar
- 1 tablespoon ground cinnamon
- 1/2 cup (1 stick) unsalted butter, softened

For the Glaze:

- 2 cups powdered sugar
- 2-4 tablespoons milk
- 1 teaspoon vanilla extract
- Green, purple, and yellow food coloring (traditional Mardi Gras colors)

Instructions:

1. In a large mixing bowl, combine the warm milk and active dry yeast. Let it sit for about 5 minutes until the yeast is dissolved and becomes frothy.
2. Add the granulated sugar, melted butter, eggs, vanilla extract, salt, nutmeg, and cinnamon to the bowl. Mix well to combine.
3. Gradually add the flour to the wet ingredients, stirring until a soft dough forms.

4. Turn the dough out onto a lightly floured surface and knead it for about 5-7 minutes until it is smooth and elastic. Alternatively, you can use a stand mixer with a dough hook attachment for this step.
5. Place the dough in a greased bowl, cover with a clean kitchen towel or plastic wrap, and let it rise in a warm place for about 1-2 hours, or until doubled in size.
6. While the dough is rising, prepare the filling by mixing together the brown sugar, granulated sugar, and ground cinnamon in a bowl. Set aside.
7. Once the dough has doubled in size, punch it down and roll it out on a lightly floured surface into a large rectangle, about 10x20 inches in size.
8. Spread the softened butter evenly over the surface of the dough rectangle, leaving about 1 inch of space along one of the long edges.
9. Sprinkle the prepared sugar-cinnamon mixture evenly over the buttered dough.
10. Starting from the opposite long edge, roll the dough up tightly into a log shape.
11. Place the rolled dough seam side down on a parchment-lined baking sheet and form it into a ring, pinching the ends together to seal.
12. Cover the dough ring loosely with plastic wrap and let it rise in a warm place for another 30-45 minutes, or until slightly puffed.
13. Preheat the oven to 350°F (175°C).
14. Once the dough has finished rising, bake the King Cake in the preheated oven for 25-30 minutes, or until golden brown and cooked through.
15. Remove the King Cake from the oven and let it cool completely on a wire rack.
16. While the cake is cooling, prepare the glaze by whisking together the powdered sugar, milk, and vanilla extract in a bowl until smooth. Add more milk as needed to reach your desired consistency.
17. Divide the glaze into three separate bowls. Dye one bowl of glaze green, one purple, and one yellow using food coloring.
18. Once the King Cake has cooled, drizzle the colored glazes over the top of the cake in alternating sections, creating a colorful pattern.
19. Serve the King Cake at room temperature and enjoy your festive Mardi Gras treat!

Traditionally, a small plastic baby figurine is hidden inside the King Cake before serving. The person who finds the baby in their slice is said to have good luck and is responsible for hosting the next King Cake party. If you choose to include a baby figurine, be sure to let your guests know before serving the cake.

Oysters Rockefeller

Ingredients:

- 24 fresh oysters, shucked, with their shells reserved
- 1/2 cup (1 stick) unsalted butter
- 1/2 cup finely chopped onion
- 1/2 cup finely chopped celery
- 1/2 cup finely chopped green bell pepper
- 2 cloves garlic, minced
- 1/4 cup chopped fresh parsley
- 1/4 cup chopped fresh spinach
- 1/4 cup chopped fresh fennel (optional)
- 1/4 cup Pernod or other anise-flavored liqueur (optional)
- 1/2 cup bread crumbs
- 1/4 cup grated Parmesan cheese
- Salt and black pepper to taste
- Rock salt or coarse salt, for serving

Instructions:

1. Preheat your oven to 450°F (230°C).
2. Scrub the reserved oyster shells clean under cold running water and place them on a baking sheet filled with rock salt or coarse salt to stabilize them.
3. In a large skillet, melt the butter over medium heat. Add the chopped onion, celery, and green bell pepper. Cook, stirring occasionally, until the vegetables are softened, about 5-7 minutes.
4. Add the minced garlic to the skillet and cook for an additional minute until fragrant.
5. Stir in the chopped parsley, spinach, and fennel (if using). Cook for another 2-3 minutes until the spinach is wilted.
6. If using Pernod or another anise-flavored liqueur, add it to the skillet and cook for another minute until slightly reduced.
7. Remove the skillet from the heat and stir in the bread crumbs and grated Parmesan cheese. Season the mixture with salt and black pepper to taste.
8. Place a spoonful of the vegetable mixture on top of each shucked oyster in its shell, covering the oyster completely.
9. Bake the Oysters Rockefeller in the preheated oven for about 10-12 minutes, or until the topping is golden brown and bubbling.
10. Remove the Oysters Rockefeller from the oven and let them cool slightly before serving.
11. Serve the Oysters Rockefeller hot, garnished with additional chopped parsley if desired.
12. Enjoy your delicious and indulgent Oysters Rockefeller as an elegant appetizer for any special occasion or dinner party!

Shrimp Creole

Ingredients:

- 1 lb (450g) large shrimp, peeled and deveined
- 2 tablespoons vegetable oil
- 1 onion, finely chopped
- 1 green bell pepper, finely chopped
- 2 celery stalks, finely chopped
- 3 cloves garlic, minced
- 1 can (14.5 oz) diced tomatoes
- 1 can (8 oz) tomato sauce
- 1 cup (240 ml) chicken broth or seafood broth
- 2 tablespoons tomato paste
- 1 tablespoon Worcestershire sauce
- 1 teaspoon hot sauce (adjust to taste)
- 1 teaspoon sugar
- 1 teaspoon paprika
- 1/2 teaspoon dried thyme
- 1/2 teaspoon dried oregano
- Salt and black pepper to taste
- Cooked white rice, for serving
- Chopped fresh parsley, for garnish

Instructions:

1. In a large skillet or Dutch oven, heat the vegetable oil over medium heat.
2. Add the chopped onion, green bell pepper, and celery to the skillet. Cook, stirring occasionally, until the vegetables are softened, about 5-7 minutes.
3. Add the minced garlic to the skillet and cook for an additional minute until fragrant.
4. Stir in the diced tomatoes (with their juices), tomato sauce, chicken broth, tomato paste, Worcestershire sauce, hot sauce, sugar, paprika, dried thyme, and dried oregano. Mix well to combine.
5. Bring the mixture to a simmer, then reduce the heat to low. Cover and let it simmer for about 20-25 minutes, stirring occasionally, to allow the flavors to meld together and the sauce to thicken.

6. Season the sauce with salt and black pepper to taste.
7. Add the peeled and deveined shrimp to the skillet. Cook for 5-7 minutes, or until the shrimp are pink and cooked through.
8. Taste and adjust the seasoning of the sauce if needed.
9. Serve the Shrimp Creole hot over cooked white rice.
10. Garnish with chopped fresh parsley before serving.
11. Enjoy your delicious and flavorful Shrimp Creole, a classic Creole dish that's perfect for any occasion!

Andouille Sausage

Ingredients:

- 2 lbs (about 900g) pork butt, cubed
- 1 lb (about 450g) pork fatback, cubed
- 4 cloves garlic, minced
- 2 tablespoons kosher salt
- 1 tablespoon smoked paprika
- 1 tablespoon ground black pepper
- 1 tablespoon dried thyme
- 1 tablespoon dried oregano
- 2 teaspoons cayenne pepper (adjust to taste)
- 1 teaspoon ground white pepper
- 1/2 teaspoon ground cloves
- Natural hog casings (optional, for stuffing)

Instructions:

1. In a large mixing bowl, combine the cubed pork butt and pork fatback.
2. In a small bowl, mix together the minced garlic, kosher salt, smoked paprika, black pepper, dried thyme, dried oregano, cayenne pepper, ground white pepper, and ground cloves to make the spice blend.
3. Sprinkle the spice blend over the cubed pork and fatback, making sure it is evenly distributed.
4. Cover the bowl with plastic wrap and refrigerate for at least 4 hours, or overnight, to allow the flavors to meld together.
5. Once the meat has marinated, if you're not using casings, shape the sausage mixture into patties or use it loose in recipes like jambalaya or gumbo.
6. If you're using casings, rinse them thoroughly in cold water and soak them in warm water for about 30 minutes to soften them.
7. Stuff the sausage mixture into the casings using a sausage stuffer or a funnel attached to the end of a sausage-making attachment on a stand mixer. Make sure to leave space between the sausage links to allow for expansion.
8. Twist or tie off the casings at regular intervals to form individual sausages.
9. Prick any air bubbles with a pin and gently squeeze the sausages to distribute the filling evenly.
10. If you're not cooking the sausage immediately, you can store it in the refrigerator for up to 3 days or freeze it for longer storage.
11. To cook the Andouille sausage, you can grill, pan-fry, bake, or boil it, depending on your preference and the recipe you're using it in.

12. Enjoy your homemade Andouille sausage in dishes like jambalaya, gumbo, red beans and rice, or simply grilled and served with mustard and crusty bread.

Bread Pudding with Whiskey Sauce

Bread Pudding Ingredients:

- 6 cups stale bread cubes (French bread or brioche work well)
- 2 cups whole milk
- 1 cup heavy cream
- 4 large eggs
- 1 cup granulated sugar
- 1 teaspoon vanilla extract
- 1 teaspoon ground cinnamon
- 1/4 teaspoon ground nutmeg
- 1/2 cup raisins or chopped pecans (optional)

Whiskey Sauce Ingredients:

- 1/2 cup unsalted butter
- 1 cup granulated sugar
- 1/2 cup heavy cream
- 2 tablespoons whiskey (bourbon or Irish whiskey work well)
- Pinch of salt

Instructions:

For the Bread Pudding:

1. Preheat your oven to 350°F (175°C). Grease a 9x13 inch baking dish.
2. In a large mixing bowl, whisk together the whole milk, heavy cream, eggs, granulated sugar, vanilla extract, cinnamon, and nutmeg until well combined.
3. Add the stale bread cubes to the bowl and gently toss until the bread is evenly coated in the custard mixture. Let it sit for about 10-15 minutes, stirring occasionally, to allow the bread to soak up the liquid.
4. If using, fold in the raisins or chopped pecans into the bread mixture.
5. Pour the bread mixture into the prepared baking dish, spreading it out evenly.
6. Bake in the preheated oven for 45-50 minutes, or until the top is golden brown and the custard is set.
7. Remove the bread pudding from the oven and let it cool slightly before serving.

For the Whiskey Sauce:

1. In a small saucepan, melt the unsalted butter over medium heat.
2. Add the granulated sugar and heavy cream to the saucepan, stirring constantly until the sugar is dissolved and the mixture is smooth.
3. Reduce the heat to low and simmer the sauce for about 5-7 minutes, stirring occasionally, until it thickens slightly.
4. Remove the saucepan from the heat and stir in the whiskey and a pinch of salt.
5. Let the whiskey sauce cool slightly before serving.

To Serve:

1. Cut the bread pudding into squares and serve warm.
2. Drizzle the warm whiskey sauce over the bread pudding just before serving.
3. Enjoy your delicious bread pudding with whiskey sauce as a comforting and indulgent dessert!

Turtle Soup

Ingredients:

- 2 lbs (about 900g) turtle meat, cleaned and diced (you can also use beef or veal as a substitute)
- 1/4 cup all-purpose flour
- 1/4 cup vegetable oil
- 1 large onion, diced
- 1 bell pepper, diced
- 2 celery stalks, diced
- 4 cloves garlic, minced
- 1 can (14.5 oz) diced tomatoes
- 4 cups beef broth
- 2 cups chicken broth
- 1/2 cup dry sherry
- 2 bay leaves
- 1 teaspoon dried thyme
- 1 teaspoon Worcestershire sauce
- 1 teaspoon hot sauce (adjust to taste)
- Salt and black pepper to taste
- Cooked white rice, for serving
- Chopped fresh parsley, for garnish

Instructions:

1. In a large pot or Dutch oven, heat the vegetable oil over medium heat.
2. Season the diced turtle meat with salt and black pepper, then dredge it in the all-purpose flour, shaking off any excess.
3. Add the floured turtle meat to the pot and cook until browned on all sides, about 5-7 minutes. Remove the browned meat from the pot and set it aside.
4. In the same pot, add the diced onion, bell pepper, and celery. Cook, stirring occasionally, until the vegetables are softened, about 5 minutes.
5. Add the minced garlic to the pot and cook for an additional minute until fragrant.
6. Return the browned turtle meat to the pot. Add the diced tomatoes (with their juices), beef broth, chicken broth, dry sherry, bay leaves, dried thyme, Worcestershire sauce, and hot sauce. Stir well to combine.
7. Bring the soup to a simmer, then reduce the heat to low. Cover and let it simmer for about 1-2 hours, stirring occasionally, until the turtle meat is tender.
8. Taste the soup and adjust the seasoning with more salt, black pepper, or hot sauce if needed.
9. Serve the turtle soup hot over cooked white rice.

10. Garnish each serving with chopped fresh parsley.
11. Enjoy your flavorful and comforting turtle soup, a classic dish in Creole cuisine!

Fried Alligator Bites

Ingredients:

- 1 lb (about 450g) alligator meat, cut into bite-sized pieces
- 1 cup buttermilk
- 1 tablespoon hot sauce (optional)
- 1 cup all-purpose flour
- 1 teaspoon paprika
- 1 teaspoon garlic powder
- 1 teaspoon onion powder
- 1/2 teaspoon cayenne pepper (adjust to taste)
- Salt and black pepper to taste
- Vegetable oil, for frying
- Lemon wedges, for serving
- Cocktail sauce or remoulade sauce, for dipping

Instructions:

1. In a large mixing bowl, combine the buttermilk and hot sauce (if using). Add the alligator meat pieces to the bowl and toss to coat them in the buttermilk mixture. Cover and refrigerate for at least 30 minutes, or up to 4 hours, to allow the meat to marinate.
2. In a shallow dish, combine the all-purpose flour, paprika, garlic powder, onion powder, cayenne pepper, salt, and black pepper. Mix well to combine.
3. Remove the marinated alligator meat from the refrigerator. Dredge each piece in the seasoned flour mixture, shaking off any excess.
4. Heat vegetable oil in a deep fryer or large skillet to 350°F (175°C).
5. Carefully add the breaded alligator pieces to the hot oil in batches, making sure not to overcrowd the fryer or skillet. Fry for about 3-4 minutes, or until the alligator bites are golden brown and crispy.
6. Use a slotted spoon or tongs to transfer the fried alligator bites to a plate lined with paper towels to drain excess oil.
7. Repeat the frying process with the remaining alligator pieces.
8. Serve the fried alligator bites hot, garnished with lemon wedges.
9. Serve with cocktail sauce or remoulade sauce on the side for dipping.
10. Enjoy your crispy and delicious fried alligator bites as an appetizer or snack!

Crab Cakes

Ingredients:

- 1 lb (about 450g) lump crab meat, drained well
- 1/2 cup mayonnaise
- 1 large egg
- 1 tablespoon Dijon mustard
- 1 tablespoon Worcestershire sauce
- 1 tablespoon lemon juice
- 1 teaspoon Old Bay seasoning
- 1/4 cup chopped fresh parsley
- 1/4 cup chopped green onions (scallions)
- 1 cup breadcrumbs
- Salt and black pepper to taste
- 2-3 tablespoons vegetable oil, for frying
- Lemon wedges and tartar sauce, for serving

Instructions:

1. In a large mixing bowl, combine the mayonnaise, egg, Dijon mustard, Worcestershire sauce, lemon juice, Old Bay seasoning, chopped parsley, and chopped green onions. Mix well.
2. Gently fold in the lump crab meat until well combined, being careful not to break up the crab meat too much.
3. Gradually add the breadcrumbs to the mixture, stirring until the mixture holds together. You may need to adjust the amount of breadcrumbs depending on the moisture content of the crab meat.
4. Season the mixture with salt and black pepper to taste.
5. Shape the crab mixture into round patties, about 1/2 inch thick. Place the patties on a baking sheet lined with parchment paper and refrigerate for at least 30 minutes to firm up.
6. Heat vegetable oil in a large skillet over medium heat.
7. Once the oil is hot, carefully add the crab cakes to the skillet in batches, being careful not to overcrowd the pan. Cook the crab cakes for about 4-5 minutes on each side, or until golden brown and crispy.
8. Use a spatula to carefully flip the crab cakes and cook for an additional 4-5 minutes on the other side.
9. Once cooked, transfer the crab cakes to a plate lined with paper towels to drain any excess oil.
10. Serve the crab cakes hot with lemon wedges and tartar sauce on the side.
11. Enjoy your delicious homemade crab cakes as a flavorful appetizer or main dish!

Dirty Rice

Ingredients:

- 1 lb (about 450g) ground pork or chicken
- 1 cup white rice
- 2 cups chicken broth
- 2 tablespoons vegetable oil
- 1 onion, finely chopped
- 1 bell pepper, finely chopped
- 2 celery stalks, finely chopped
- 3 cloves garlic, minced
- 2 green onions (scallions), chopped
- 2 tablespoons Cajun seasoning
- 1 teaspoon paprika
- 1/2 teaspoon dried thyme
- Salt and black pepper to taste
- Chopped fresh parsley, for garnish (optional)

Instructions:

1. In a large skillet or Dutch oven, heat the vegetable oil over medium heat.
2. Add the ground pork or chicken to the skillet and cook, breaking it up with a spoon, until browned and cooked through, about 5-7 minutes.
3. Remove the cooked meat from the skillet and set it aside.
4. In the same skillet, add the chopped onion, bell pepper, and celery. Cook, stirring occasionally, until the vegetables are softened, about 5 minutes.
5. Add the minced garlic to the skillet and cook for an additional minute until fragrant.
6. Return the cooked meat to the skillet with the vegetables.
7. Stir in the white rice, Cajun seasoning, paprika, and dried thyme until well combined.
8. Pour the chicken broth into the skillet and stir to combine all the ingredients.
9. Bring the mixture to a simmer, then reduce the heat to low. Cover and let it cook for about 15-20 minutes, or until the rice is tender and has absorbed most of the liquid.
10. Once the rice is cooked, taste and adjust the seasoning with salt and black pepper if needed.
11. Stir in the chopped green onions (scallions) just before serving.
12. Garnish the Dirty Rice with chopped fresh parsley, if desired.
13. Serve hot as a side dish or as a main course.
14. Enjoy your flavorful and satisfying Dirty Rice, packed with Cajun spices and hearty goodness!

Cajun Fried Chicken

Ingredients:

- 4 bone-in, skin-on chicken thighs
- 4 bone-in, skin-on chicken drumsticks
- 2 cups buttermilk
- 2 tablespoons hot sauce (optional)
- 2 cups all-purpose flour
- 2 tablespoons Cajun seasoning
- 1 teaspoon paprika
- 1 teaspoon garlic powder
- 1 teaspoon onion powder
- 1/2 teaspoon cayenne pepper (adjust to taste)
- Salt and black pepper to taste
- Vegetable oil, for frying

Instructions:

1. In a large mixing bowl, combine the buttermilk and hot sauce (if using). Add the chicken pieces to the bowl and toss to coat them in the buttermilk mixture. Cover and refrigerate for at least 4 hours, or overnight, to allow the chicken to marinate.
2. In a shallow dish, combine the all-purpose flour, Cajun seasoning, paprika, garlic powder, onion powder, cayenne pepper, salt, and black pepper. Mix well to combine.
3. Remove the marinated chicken from the refrigerator and let it sit at room temperature for about 30 minutes.
4. Heat vegetable oil in a deep fryer or large skillet to 350°F (175°C).
5. Remove the chicken pieces from the buttermilk marinade, shaking off any excess.
6. Dredge each chicken piece in the seasoned flour mixture, pressing down gently to adhere the flour to the chicken.
7. Carefully add the breaded chicken pieces to the hot oil in batches, making sure not to overcrowd the fryer or skillet. Fry for about 12-15 minutes, or until the chicken is golden brown and cooked through, with an internal temperature of 165°F (75°C).
8. Use a slotted spoon or tongs to transfer the fried chicken pieces to a plate lined with paper towels to drain excess oil.
9. Repeat the frying process with the remaining chicken pieces.
10. Let the fried chicken rest for a few minutes before serving.
11. Serve the Cajun Fried Chicken hot, with your favorite side dishes like mashed potatoes, coleslaw, cornbread, or macaroni and cheese.
12. Enjoy your flavorful and crispy Cajun Fried Chicken, packed with the bold flavors of Cajun seasoning!

Maque Choux (Corn and Peppers)

Ingredients:

- 4 cups fresh or frozen corn kernels
- 1 tablespoon vegetable oil or bacon fat
- 1 onion, diced
- 1 bell pepper, diced
- 2 cloves garlic, minced
- 1 cup diced tomatoes (fresh or canned)
- 1/2 cup chicken broth or vegetable broth
- 1 teaspoon Cajun seasoning
- 1/2 teaspoon paprika
- Salt and black pepper to taste
- Chopped fresh parsley or green onions (scallions), for garnish (optional)

Instructions:

1. Heat the vegetable oil or bacon fat in a large skillet or Dutch oven over medium heat.
2. Add the diced onion and bell pepper to the skillet. Cook, stirring occasionally, until the vegetables are softened, about 5 minutes.
3. Add the minced garlic to the skillet and cook for an additional minute until fragrant.
4. Stir in the corn kernels and diced tomatoes. Cook for another 3-4 minutes, stirring occasionally.
5. Pour in the chicken broth and stir to combine.
6. Season the mixture with Cajun seasoning, paprika, salt, and black pepper to taste. Adjust the seasoning according to your preference.
7. Reduce the heat to low and let the Maque Choux simmer for about 10-15 minutes, stirring occasionally, until the flavors are well combined and the mixture has thickened slightly.
8. Once cooked, taste and adjust the seasoning if needed.
9. Garnish the Maque Choux with chopped fresh parsley or green onions (scallions) before serving, if desired.
10. Serve the Maque Choux hot as a flavorful side dish, or enjoy it on its own as a light and delicious meal!
11. Enjoy the bold flavors of this classic Cajun dish, perfect for any occasion!

Pralines

Ingredients:

- 1 cup granulated sugar
- 1 cup packed brown sugar
- 1/2 cup heavy cream
- 1/4 cup unsalted butter
- 1 teaspoon vanilla extract
- 1 1/2 cups pecan halves

Instructions:

1. Line a baking sheet with parchment paper or a silicone baking mat and set aside.
2. In a medium saucepan, combine the granulated sugar, brown sugar, heavy cream, and unsalted butter.
3. Cook the mixture over medium heat, stirring constantly, until the sugars are dissolved and the mixture comes to a boil.
4. Continue to cook the mixture, stirring occasionally, until it reaches 238°F (114°C) on a candy thermometer, or until a small amount of the mixture forms a soft ball when dropped into cold water.
5. Once the mixture reaches the desired temperature, remove the saucepan from the heat and stir in the vanilla extract and pecan halves.
6. Let the mixture cool for a few minutes, stirring occasionally, until it thickens slightly and begins to lose its gloss.
7. Working quickly, use a spoon to drop small mounds of the praline mixture onto the prepared baking sheet, spacing them a few inches apart.
8. Let the pralines cool completely at room temperature until they are firm and set.
9. Once cooled, store the pralines in an airtight container at room temperature for up to 1 week.
10. Enjoy your homemade pralines as a sweet and nutty treat, perfect for snacking or gifting to friends and family!

Cajun Shrimp Pasta

Ingredients:

- 8 oz (225g) pasta (such as fettuccine or penne)
- 1 lb (about 450g) large shrimp, peeled and deveined
- 2 tablespoons Cajun seasoning
- 2 tablespoons olive oil
- 4 cloves garlic, minced
- 1 onion, diced
- 1 bell pepper, diced
- 1 cup cherry tomatoes, halved
- 1 cup heavy cream
- 1/2 cup chicken broth or seafood broth
- 1 teaspoon paprika
- Salt and black pepper to taste
- Chopped fresh parsley, for garnish
- Grated Parmesan cheese, for serving (optional)

Instructions:

1. Cook the pasta according to the package instructions until al dente. Drain and set aside.
2. In a mixing bowl, toss the peeled and deveined shrimp with Cajun seasoning until evenly coated.
3. Heat olive oil in a large skillet over medium-high heat. Add the seasoned shrimp to the skillet and cook for 2-3 minutes per side, or until they are pink and cooked through. Remove the shrimp from the skillet and set aside.
4. In the same skillet, add the minced garlic, diced onion, and diced bell pepper. Cook, stirring occasionally, until the vegetables are softened, about 5 minutes.
5. Add the halved cherry tomatoes to the skillet and cook for another 2-3 minutes, until they start to soften.
6. Pour in the heavy cream and chicken broth, stirring to combine. Bring the mixture to a simmer.
7. Stir in the paprika, salt, and black pepper to taste. Simmer for 3-4 minutes, until the sauce thickens slightly.
8. Add the cooked pasta to the skillet, tossing to coat it in the creamy Cajun sauce.
9. Return the cooked shrimp to the skillet, stirring gently to combine with the pasta and sauce.
10. Cook for an additional 2-3 minutes, or until everything is heated through.
11. Remove the skillet from the heat and garnish the Cajun shrimp pasta with chopped fresh parsley.
12. Serve hot, with grated Parmesan cheese on the side if desired.

13. Enjoy your delicious and flavorful Cajun shrimp pasta!

Cajun Shrimp and Grits

Ingredients:

For the Shrimp:

- 1 lb (about 450g) large shrimp, peeled and deveined
- 2 tablespoons Cajun seasoning
- 2 tablespoons olive oil
- 4 cloves garlic, minced
- 1 bell pepper, diced
- 1 onion, diced
- 1 cup diced tomatoes (fresh or canned)
- 1 cup chicken broth
- 1/2 cup heavy cream
- Salt and black pepper to taste
- Chopped fresh parsley, for garnish

For the Grits:

- 1 cup stone-ground grits
- 4 cups water
- 1 cup milk
- 4 tablespoons unsalted butter
- Salt to taste
- Grated cheddar cheese, for serving (optional)

Instructions:

1. In a large bowl, toss the peeled and deveined shrimp with Cajun seasoning until evenly coated. Set aside.
2. In a large skillet, heat olive oil over medium-high heat. Add the seasoned shrimp and cook for 2-3 minutes per side, until pink and cooked through. Remove the shrimp from the skillet and set aside.
3. In the same skillet, add minced garlic, diced bell pepper, and diced onion. Cook until the vegetables are softened, about 5 minutes.
4. Add diced tomatoes to the skillet and cook for an additional 2-3 minutes.
5. Pour in chicken broth and heavy cream, stirring to combine. Bring the mixture to a simmer.

6. Season with salt and black pepper to taste. Simmer for 5-7 minutes, until the sauce thickens slightly.
7. While the sauce is simmering, prepare the grits. In a medium saucepan, bring water and milk to a boil. Stir in grits and reduce heat to low. Cook, stirring occasionally, for 20-25 minutes, or until the grits are creamy and tender.
8. Stir in butter and salt to taste into the cooked grits.
9. Serve the Cajun shrimp over a bed of creamy grits. Garnish with chopped parsley and grated cheddar cheese if desired.
10. Enjoy your flavorful Cajun shrimp and grits!

Catfish Courtbouillon

Ingredients:

- 4 catfish fillets, about 6-8 ounces each
- Salt and black pepper to taste
- 1/4 cup vegetable oil
- 1 onion, finely chopped
- 1 bell pepper, finely chopped
- 2 celery stalks, finely chopped
- 3 cloves garlic, minced
- 1 can (14.5 oz) diced tomatoes
- 1 cup seafood or chicken broth
- 1/2 cup tomato sauce
- 1 tablespoon Worcestershire sauce
- 1 tablespoon hot sauce (adjust to taste)
- 1 teaspoon Cajun seasoning
- 1/2 teaspoon paprika
- 1/4 teaspoon dried thyme
- 1/4 teaspoon dried oregano
- 1 bay leaf
- Chopped fresh parsley, for garnish
- Cooked white rice, for serving

Instructions:

1. Season the catfish fillets with salt and black pepper to taste.
2. Heat vegetable oil in a large skillet or Dutch oven over medium-high heat.
3. Add the seasoned catfish fillets to the skillet and cook for 3-4 minutes on each side, until lightly browned. Remove the catfish from the skillet and set aside.
4. In the same skillet, add chopped onion, bell pepper, and celery. Cook, stirring occasionally, until the vegetables are softened, about 5-7 minutes.
5. Add minced garlic to the skillet and cook for an additional minute until fragrant.
6. Stir in diced tomatoes (with their juices), seafood or chicken broth, tomato sauce, Worcestershire sauce, hot sauce, Cajun seasoning, paprika, dried thyme, dried oregano, and bay leaf. Mix well to combine.
7. Bring the mixture to a simmer, then reduce the heat to low. Cover and let it simmer for about 15-20 minutes, stirring occasionally, to allow the flavors to meld together.
8. Return the cooked catfish fillets to the skillet, nestling them into the sauce. Cover and let them simmer for another 10-15 minutes, or until the catfish is cooked through and flakes easily with a fork.
9. Taste and adjust the seasoning of the sauce if needed.

10. Serve the catfish courtbouillon hot over cooked white rice.
11. Garnish with chopped fresh parsley before serving.
12. Enjoy your delicious and flavorful catfish courtbouillon, a classic Louisiana dish packed with bold flavors!

Blackened Fish (Redfish or Catfish)

Ingredients:

- 4 fish fillets (redfish or catfish), about 6-8 ounces each
- 4 tablespoons unsalted butter, melted
- 2 tablespoons Cajun seasoning
- 1 teaspoon paprika
- 1 teaspoon garlic powder
- 1 teaspoon onion powder
- 1/2 teaspoon dried thyme
- 1/2 teaspoon dried oregano
- 1/2 teaspoon black pepper
- 1/2 teaspoon cayenne pepper (adjust to taste)
- Salt to taste
- Vegetable oil, for cooking
- Lemon wedges, for serving
- Chopped fresh parsley, for garnish

Instructions:

1. In a small bowl, combine Cajun seasoning, paprika, garlic powder, onion powder, dried thyme, dried oregano, black pepper, cayenne pepper, and salt to taste.
2. Pat the fish fillets dry with paper towels and then brush both sides with melted butter.
3. Generously coat both sides of each fish fillet with the spice mixture.
4. Heat a large skillet over high heat until very hot.
5. Add a small amount of vegetable oil to the skillet to prevent sticking.
6. Carefully place the seasoned fish fillets in the skillet, skin side down if using skin-on fillets.
7. Cook for 2-3 minutes on each side, or until the spices form a blackened crust and the fish is cooked through.
8. Transfer the blackened fish to a serving plate.
9. Garnish with chopped fresh parsley and serve with lemon wedges on the side.
10. Enjoy your delicious blackened fish as a flavorful and spicy Cajun-inspired dish!

Cajun Crab Dip

Ingredients:

- 8 oz (225g) lump crab meat, drained
- 8 oz (225g) cream cheese, softened
- 1/2 cup mayonnaise
- 1/4 cup sour cream
- 1 cup shredded cheddar cheese
- 1/4 cup grated Parmesan cheese
- 1 tablespoon Cajun seasoning
- 1 teaspoon hot sauce (adjust to taste)
- 2 cloves garlic, minced
- 2 green onions, thinly sliced
- Salt and black pepper to taste
- Chopped fresh parsley, for garnish (optional)
- Crackers, bread, or vegetables, for serving

Instructions:

1. Preheat your oven to 375°F (190°C).
2. In a large mixing bowl, combine the softened cream cheese, mayonnaise, sour cream, shredded cheddar cheese, grated Parmesan cheese, Cajun seasoning, hot sauce, minced garlic, and sliced green onions. Mix until well combined.
3. Gently fold in the lump crab meat, being careful not to break it up too much.
4. Season the mixture with salt and black pepper to taste.
5. Transfer the Cajun crab dip mixture to a baking dish or oven-safe skillet, spreading it out evenly.
6. Bake in the preheated oven for 20-25 minutes, or until the dip is hot and bubbly and the top is lightly golden brown.
7. Remove the dip from the oven and let it cool for a few minutes.
8. Garnish with chopped fresh parsley, if desired, before serving.
9. Serve the Cajun crab dip hot with crackers, bread, or vegetables for dipping.
10. Enjoy your creamy and flavorful Cajun crab dip as a delicious appetizer for parties or gatherings!

Creole Tomato Salad

Ingredients:

- 4 large ripe Creole tomatoes, sliced
- 1 small red onion, thinly sliced
- 1/4 cup extra virgin olive oil
- 2 tablespoons red wine vinegar
- 1 clove garlic, minced
- 1 tablespoon chopped fresh basil
- 1 tablespoon chopped fresh parsley
- 1 teaspoon sugar (optional)
- Salt and black pepper to taste
- Crumbled feta cheese or fresh mozzarella (optional), for garnish
- Fresh basil leaves, for garnish

Instructions:

1. Arrange the sliced Creole tomatoes and red onion slices on a serving platter.
2. In a small bowl, whisk together the extra virgin olive oil, red wine vinegar, minced garlic, chopped fresh basil, chopped fresh parsley, sugar (if using), salt, and black pepper to make the dressing.
3. Drizzle the dressing over the sliced tomatoes and red onions.
4. Gently toss to coat the tomatoes and onions in the dressing.
5. Let the tomato salad marinate for at least 15-20 minutes at room temperature to allow the flavors to meld together.
6. Just before serving, garnish the tomato salad with crumbled feta cheese or fresh mozzarella (if using) and fresh basil leaves.
7. Serve the Creole tomato salad as a refreshing side dish or appetizer.
8. Enjoy the vibrant flavors of ripe tomatoes in this simple and delicious Creole tomato salad!

Cajun Cornbread

Ingredients:

- 1 cup yellow cornmeal
- 1 cup all-purpose flour
- 1 tablespoon baking powder
- 1 teaspoon salt
- 1/2 teaspoon Cajun seasoning
- 1/2 teaspoon garlic powder
- 1/2 teaspoon onion powder
- 1/4 teaspoon cayenne pepper (adjust to taste)
- 1 cup buttermilk
- 2 large eggs
- 1/4 cup unsalted butter, melted
- 1/4 cup canned cream-style corn (optional)
- 1/2 cup shredded cheddar cheese (optional)
- 2-3 slices cooked bacon, crumbled (optional)
- Chopped green onions (scallions) for garnish (optional)

Instructions:

1. Preheat your oven to 400°F (200°C). Grease a 9-inch square baking dish or cast iron skillet.
2. In a large mixing bowl, combine the yellow cornmeal, all-purpose flour, baking powder, salt, Cajun seasoning, garlic powder, onion powder, and cayenne pepper. Mix well.
3. In a separate bowl, whisk together the buttermilk, eggs, and melted butter until well combined.
4. Pour the wet ingredients into the dry ingredients and stir until just combined. Be careful not to overmix.
5. If desired, fold in the cream-style corn, shredded cheddar cheese, and crumbled bacon until evenly distributed throughout the batter.
6. Pour the batter into the prepared baking dish or skillet, spreading it out evenly.
7. Bake in the preheated oven for 20-25 minutes, or until the cornbread is golden brown and a toothpick inserted into the center comes out clean.
8. Remove the cornbread from the oven and let it cool in the pan for a few minutes before slicing.
9. Garnish with chopped green onions (scallions) if desired.
10. Serve the Cajun cornbread warm as a side dish or as a tasty accompaniment to soups, stews, or chili.
11. Enjoy the spicy and flavorful twist of Cajun cornbread!

Bourbon Street Chicken

Ingredients:

- 4 boneless, skinless chicken breasts
- Salt and black pepper to taste
- 2 tablespoons vegetable oil
- 1/4 cup bourbon whiskey
- 1/4 cup soy sauce
- 1/4 cup brown sugar
- 2 cloves garlic, minced
- 1 teaspoon grated fresh ginger
- 1/4 teaspoon cayenne pepper (adjust to taste)
- 1 tablespoon cornstarch
- 2 tablespoons water
- Chopped green onions (scallions) for garnish
- Cooked white rice, for serving

Instructions:

1. Season the chicken breasts with salt and black pepper to taste on both sides.
2. Heat vegetable oil in a large skillet over medium-high heat.
3. Add the seasoned chicken breasts to the skillet and cook for 5-6 minutes on each side, or until golden brown and cooked through. Remove the chicken from the skillet and set aside.
4. In the same skillet, add bourbon whiskey, soy sauce, brown sugar, minced garlic, grated ginger, and cayenne pepper. Stir to combine.
5. Bring the sauce to a simmer and let it cook for 2-3 minutes, stirring occasionally, until slightly thickened.
6. In a small bowl, mix cornstarch and water to make a slurry. Stir the slurry into the sauce and continue to cook for another 1-2 minutes, until the sauce thickens further.
7. Return the cooked chicken breasts to the skillet, turning to coat them in the bourbon sauce. Let the chicken simmer in the sauce for 2-3 minutes to heat through and absorb the flavors.
8. Garnish the Bourbon Street chicken with chopped green onions (scallions) before serving.
9. Serve hot over cooked white rice.

10. Enjoy your flavorful and savory Bourbon Street chicken, reminiscent of the vibrant flavors of New Orleans cuisine!

Mirliton Casserole

Ingredients:

- 4 mirliton squash (chayote), peeled and diced
- 1 onion, diced
- 2 cloves garlic, minced
- 1 bell pepper, diced
- 2 stalks celery, diced
- 1/4 cup butter
- 1 cup breadcrumbs
- 1 cup cooked and shredded chicken or shrimp (optional)
- 1/2 cup grated Parmesan cheese
- 1/4 cup chopped fresh parsley
- 1/4 cup chopped green onions (scallions)
- 2 eggs, beaten
- Salt and black pepper to taste
- Cooking spray or butter, for greasing the baking dish

Instructions:

1. Preheat your oven to 350°F (175°C). Grease a 9x13-inch baking dish with cooking spray or butter.
2. Place the diced mirliton squash in a large pot and cover with water. Bring the water to a boil, then reduce the heat to medium-low and simmer for about 20-25 minutes, or until the squash is tender. Drain and set aside.
3. In a large skillet, melt the butter over medium heat. Add the diced onion, minced garlic, diced bell pepper, and diced celery. Cook, stirring occasionally, until the vegetables are softened, about 5-7 minutes.
4. Add the cooked and drained mirliton squash to the skillet with the cooked vegetables. Mash the squash slightly with a fork or potato masher, leaving some texture.
5. Stir in the breadcrumbs, cooked and shredded chicken or shrimp (if using), grated Parmesan cheese, chopped fresh parsley, chopped green onions, and beaten eggs. Mix until all ingredients are well combined. Season with salt and black pepper to taste.
6. Transfer the mixture to the prepared baking dish, spreading it out evenly.
7. Bake in the preheated oven for 30-35 minutes, or until the top is golden brown and the casserole is set.
8. Remove the casserole from the oven and let it cool for a few minutes before serving.
9. Serve the mirliton casserole warm as a side dish or as a main course.
10. Enjoy the delicious flavors of this classic Louisiana dish!

Seafood Gumbo

Ingredients:

- 1/2 cup vegetable oil
- 1/2 cup all-purpose flour
- 1 onion, diced
- 1 bell pepper, diced
- 2 celery stalks, diced
- 4 cloves garlic, minced
- 1 can (14.5 oz) diced tomatoes
- 6 cups seafood or chicken broth
- 1 lb (about 450g) shrimp, peeled and deveined
- 1 lb (about 450g) crabmeat
- 1 lb (about 450g) crawfish tails, peeled
- 1 lb (about 450g) okra, sliced (fresh or frozen)
- 2 bay leaves
- 1 teaspoon dried thyme
- 1 teaspoon dried oregano
- 1/2 teaspoon cayenne pepper (adjust to taste)
- Salt and black pepper to taste
- Cooked white rice, for serving
- Chopped green onions (scallions) for garnish

Instructions:

1. In a large Dutch oven or heavy-bottomed pot, heat the vegetable oil over medium heat. Gradually whisk in the flour to make a roux. Cook, stirring constantly, until the roux is a dark caramel color, about 20-30 minutes. Be careful not to burn it.
2. Add the diced onion, bell pepper, celery, and minced garlic to the pot. Cook, stirring occasionally, until the vegetables are softened, about 5-7 minutes.
3. Stir in the diced tomatoes and cook for another 2-3 minutes.
4. Gradually pour in the seafood or chicken broth, stirring to combine and scraping up any browned bits from the bottom of the pot.
5. Add the peeled and deveined shrimp, crabmeat, crawfish tails, sliced okra, bay leaves, dried thyme, dried oregano, and cayenne pepper to the pot. Season with salt and black pepper to taste.

6. Bring the gumbo to a simmer, then reduce the heat to low. Cover and let it simmer for about 30-40 minutes, stirring occasionally, until the flavors are well combined and the seafood is cooked through.
7. Taste and adjust the seasoning of the gumbo if needed.
8. Remove the bay leaves from the gumbo before serving.
9. Serve the seafood gumbo hot over cooked white rice.
10. Garnish with chopped green onions (scallions) before serving.
11. Enjoy your delicious and flavorful seafood gumbo, a classic Louisiana favorite!

Cajun Shrimp Etouffee

Ingredients:

- 1/2 cup unsalted butter
- 1/2 cup all-purpose flour
- 1 onion, finely chopped
- 1 bell pepper, finely chopped
- 2 celery stalks, finely chopped
- 4 cloves garlic, minced
- 1 can (14.5 oz) diced tomatoes
- 2 cups seafood or chicken broth
- 1 tablespoon Cajun seasoning
- 1 teaspoon paprika
- 1/2 teaspoon dried thyme
- 1/2 teaspoon dried oregano
- 1/4 teaspoon cayenne pepper (adjust to taste)
- Salt and black pepper to taste
- 1 lb (about 450g) large shrimp, peeled and deveined
- Cooked white rice, for serving
- Chopped green onions (scallions) for garnish
- Chopped fresh parsley for garnish

Instructions:

1. In a large skillet or Dutch oven, melt the butter over medium heat.
2. Gradually whisk in the flour to make a roux. Cook, stirring constantly, until the roux is a dark caramel color, about 20-30 minutes. Be careful not to burn it.
3. Add the chopped onion, bell pepper, celery, and minced garlic to the skillet. Cook, stirring occasionally, until the vegetables are softened, about 5-7 minutes.
4. Stir in the diced tomatoes and cook for another 2-3 minutes.
5. Gradually pour in the seafood or chicken broth, stirring to combine and scraping up any browned bits from the bottom of the skillet.
6. Add the Cajun seasoning, paprika, dried thyme, dried oregano, cayenne pepper, salt, and black pepper to the skillet. Mix well.
7. Bring the mixture to a simmer, then reduce the heat to low. Cover and let it simmer for about 20-25 minutes, stirring occasionally, to allow the flavors to meld together and the sauce to thicken.
8. Add the peeled and deveined shrimp to the skillet. Cook for 5-7 minutes, or until the shrimp are pink and cooked through.
9. Taste and adjust the seasoning of the étouffée if needed.
10. Serve the Cajun Shrimp Étouffée hot over cooked white rice.

11. Garnish with chopped green onions (scallions) and chopped fresh parsley before serving.
12. Enjoy your flavorful and comforting Cajun Shrimp Étouffée!

Redfish Courtbouillon

Ingredients:

- 4 redfish fillets, about 6-8 ounces each
- Salt and black pepper to taste
- 2 tablespoons vegetable oil
- 1 onion, finely chopped
- 1 bell pepper, finely chopped
- 2 celery stalks, finely chopped
- 3 cloves garlic, minced
- 1 can (14.5 oz) diced tomatoes
- 1 cup seafood or chicken broth
- 1/4 cup tomato paste
- 1 tablespoon Cajun seasoning
- 1 teaspoon dried thyme
- 1 teaspoon dried oregano
- 1/4 teaspoon cayenne pepper (adjust to taste)
- 2 bay leaves
- Chopped fresh parsley for garnish
- Cooked white rice, for serving

Instructions:

1. Season the redfish fillets with salt and black pepper to taste on both sides.
2. In a large skillet or Dutch oven, heat the vegetable oil over medium heat.
3. Add the chopped onion, bell pepper, and celery to the skillet. Cook, stirring occasionally, until the vegetables are softened, about 5-7 minutes.
4. Stir in the minced garlic and cook for an additional minute until fragrant.
5. Add the diced tomatoes (with their juices), seafood or chicken broth, tomato paste, Cajun seasoning, dried thyme, dried oregano, cayenne pepper, and bay leaves to the skillet. Mix well to combine.
6. Bring the mixture to a simmer, then reduce the heat to low. Cover and let it simmer for about 15-20 minutes, stirring occasionally, to allow the flavors to meld together.
7. Once the sauce has simmered and thickened slightly, carefully add the redfish fillets to the skillet, nestling them into the sauce.
8. Cover and let the redfish simmer in the sauce for about 10-15 minutes, or until the fish is cooked through and flakes easily with a fork.
9. Taste and adjust the seasoning of the courtbouillon if needed.
10. Remove the bay leaves from the skillet before serving.
11. Serve the redfish courtbouillon hot over cooked white rice.
12. Garnish with chopped fresh parsley before serving.

13. Enjoy your flavorful and comforting redfish courtbouillon, a classic Louisiana favorite!

Chicken and Sausage Gumbo

Ingredients:

- 1/2 cup vegetable oil
- 1/2 cup all-purpose flour
- 1 onion, chopped
- 1 bell pepper, chopped
- 2 celery stalks, chopped
- 4 cloves garlic, minced
- 1 lb (about 450g) andouille sausage, sliced
- 4 boneless, skinless chicken thighs, cut into bite-sized pieces
- 6 cups chicken broth
- 1 can (14.5 oz) diced tomatoes
- 1 cup frozen okra, sliced (optional)
- 2 bay leaves
- 1 teaspoon dried thyme
- 1 teaspoon dried oregano
- 1/2 teaspoon cayenne pepper (adjust to taste)
- Salt and black pepper to taste
- Cooked white rice, for serving
- Chopped green onions (scallions) for garnish

Instructions:

1. In a large Dutch oven or heavy-bottomed pot, heat the vegetable oil over medium heat.
2. Gradually whisk in the flour to make a roux. Cook, stirring constantly, until the roux is a dark caramel color, about 20-30 minutes. Be careful not to burn it.
3. Add the chopped onion, bell pepper, celery, and minced garlic to the pot. Cook, stirring occasionally, until the vegetables are softened, about 5-7 minutes.
4. Stir in the sliced andouille sausage and chicken pieces. Cook, stirring occasionally, until the chicken is browned on all sides.
5. Gradually pour in the chicken broth, stirring to combine and scraping up any browned bits from the bottom of the pot.
6. Add the diced tomatoes, frozen okra (if using), bay leaves, dried thyme, dried oregano, and cayenne pepper to the pot. Season with salt and black pepper to taste.
7. Bring the gumbo to a simmer, then reduce the heat to low. Cover and let it simmer for about 1-1.5 hours, stirring occasionally, to allow the flavors to meld together and the gumbo to thicken.
8. Taste and adjust the seasoning of the gumbo if needed.
9. Serve the chicken and sausage gumbo hot over cooked white rice.
10. Garnish with chopped green onions (scallions) before serving.

11. Enjoy your flavorful and comforting chicken and sausage gumbo, a classic Cajun favorite!

Cajun Crawfish Pie

Ingredients:

For the Filling:

- 2 tablespoons unsalted butter
- 1 onion, diced
- 1 bell pepper, diced
- 2 celery stalks, diced
- 2 cloves garlic, minced
- 1 lb (about 450g) crawfish tails, peeled and deveined
- 1 cup chicken or seafood broth
- 1/2 cup heavy cream
- 2 tablespoons Cajun seasoning
- Salt and black pepper to taste
- 2 tablespoons chopped fresh parsley
- 1 tablespoon chopped green onions (scallions)
- 1 tablespoon cornstarch (optional, for thickening)

For the Pastry Crust:

- 1 1/2 cups all-purpose flour
- 1/2 teaspoon salt
- 1/2 cup cold unsalted butter, cubed
- 4-6 tablespoons ice water

Instructions:

1. Preheat your oven to 375°F (190°C).
2. To make the filling, melt the butter in a large skillet over medium heat. Add the diced onion, bell pepper, and celery. Cook, stirring occasionally, until the vegetables are softened, about 5-7 minutes.
3. Add the minced garlic to the skillet and cook for another minute until fragrant.
4. Stir in the crawfish tails and cook for 2-3 minutes, until they are heated through.
5. Pour in the chicken or seafood broth and heavy cream. Season with Cajun seasoning, salt, and black pepper to taste. Bring the mixture to a simmer and let it cook for 5-7 minutes to allow the flavors to meld together. If you prefer a thicker filling, you can mix the cornstarch with a tablespoon of water and stir it into the filling to thicken it.

6. Remove the skillet from the heat and stir in the chopped fresh parsley and green onions. Set aside to cool slightly.
7. To make the pastry crust, in a large mixing bowl, combine the all-purpose flour and salt. Add the cold cubed butter and use a pastry cutter or your fingertips to mix until the mixture resembles coarse crumbs.
8. Gradually add the ice water, one tablespoon at a time, mixing until the dough comes together. Be careful not to overwork the dough.
9. Transfer the dough to a lightly floured surface and gently knead it a few times until it forms a smooth ball. Divide the dough in half.
10. Roll out one half of the dough into a circle large enough to line the bottom and sides of a 9-inch pie dish. Trim any excess dough hanging over the edges.
11. Pour the cooled crawfish filling into the prepared pie crust.
12. Roll out the remaining half of the dough into a circle large enough to cover the top of the pie. Place it over the filling and press the edges to seal. Trim any excess dough and crimp the edges with a fork or your fingers to create a decorative border.
13. Use a sharp knife to make a few small slits in the top crust to allow steam to escape during baking.
14. Bake the crawfish pie in the preheated oven for 30-35 minutes, or until the crust is golden brown and the filling is bubbling.
15. Remove the pie from the oven and let it cool for a few minutes before serving.
16. Slice and serve the Cajun crawfish pie warm, garnished with additional chopped parsley or green onions if desired.
17. Enjoy your delicious Cajun crawfish pie!

Cajun Shrimp and Crab Boil

Ingredients:

For the Boil:

- 4 quarts water
- 1 lemon, halved
- 2 onions, quartered
- 4 cloves garlic, smashed
- 2 bay leaves
- 2 tablespoons Cajun seasoning
- 1 tablespoon Old Bay seasoning
- 1 tablespoon whole black peppercorns
- 1 teaspoon cayenne pepper (adjust to taste)
- 1 teaspoon dried thyme
- Salt to taste
- 2 lbs large shrimp, shell-on
- 1 lb crab legs, thawed if frozen

For Serving (Optional):

- Melted butter
- Cocktail sauce
- Lemon wedges
- Corn on the cob, halved
- Red potatoes, halved

Instructions:

1. In a large stockpot, combine the water, lemon halves, quartered onions, smashed garlic cloves, bay leaves, Cajun seasoning, Old Bay seasoning, black peppercorns, cayenne pepper, dried thyme, and salt to taste. Bring the mixture to a boil over high heat.
2. Once the water is boiling, reduce the heat to medium and let the boil simmer for 10-15 minutes to allow the flavors to meld together.
3. Add the red potatoes and halved corn on the cob to the pot. Let them cook for about 10 minutes, until they are just tender.
4. Add the crab legs to the pot and let them cook for about 5-7 minutes, until they are heated through.

5. Finally, add the shrimp to the pot and cook for 2-3 minutes, until they turn pink and are cooked through. Be careful not to overcook the shrimp, as they can become tough.
6. Once the seafood is cooked, turn off the heat and carefully remove the seafood, potatoes, and corn from the pot using a slotted spoon or strainer. Discard the lemon halves, onions, garlic, and bay leaves.
7. Serve the Cajun shrimp and crab boil hot on a large platter or directly on a table covered with newspaper or butcher paper for easy cleanup.
8. If desired, serve the seafood boil with melted butter, cocktail sauce, and lemon wedges on the side for dipping.
9. Enjoy your delicious and flavorful Cajun shrimp and crab boil with family and friends!

Note: Feel free to customize the seafood boil by adding other seafood such as crawfish, mussels, or clams, and adjusting the seasoning to your taste preferences.

New Orleans BBQ Shrimp

Ingredients:

- 2 lbs large shrimp, peeled and deveined
- 1/2 cup unsalted butter
- 1/4 cup Worcestershire sauce
- 1/4 cup hot sauce (such as Tabasco)
- 4 cloves garlic, minced
- 2 tablespoons Creole seasoning
- 1 tablespoon lemon juice
- 1 tablespoon chopped fresh parsley
- Crusty French bread, for serving

Instructions:

1. In a large skillet or sauté pan, melt the butter over medium heat.
2. Once the butter is melted, add the Worcestershire sauce, hot sauce, minced garlic, and Creole seasoning to the skillet. Stir to combine.
3. Bring the sauce to a simmer and let it cook for 2-3 minutes, stirring occasionally.
4. Add the peeled and deveined shrimp to the skillet, stirring to coat them in the sauce.
5. Cook the shrimp in the sauce for 5-7 minutes, or until they are pink and cooked through, stirring occasionally.
6. Once the shrimp are cooked, remove the skillet from the heat.
7. Stir in the lemon juice and chopped fresh parsley.
8. Serve the New Orleans BBQ shrimp hot, straight from the skillet, with crusty French bread for dipping into the flavorful sauce.
9. Enjoy your delicious and spicy New Orleans BBQ shrimp as a flavorful appetizer or main course!

Cajun Corn Maque Choux

Ingredients:

- 4 cups fresh corn kernels (about 6-8 ears of corn)
- 1 onion, diced
- 1 bell pepper, diced
- 2 celery stalks, diced
- 2 cloves garlic, minced
- 4 slices bacon, chopped
- 1 tablespoon vegetable oil
- 1 tablespoon butter
- 1 tablespoon Cajun seasoning
- 1/2 teaspoon paprika
- 1/4 teaspoon cayenne pepper (adjust to taste)
- Salt and black pepper to taste
- 1/2 cup chicken or vegetable broth
- Chopped fresh parsley for garnish

Instructions:

1. In a large skillet or sauté pan, cook the chopped bacon over medium heat until crisp. Remove the bacon from the pan and set aside, leaving the bacon grease in the pan.
2. Add the vegetable oil and butter to the skillet with the bacon grease. Add the diced onion, bell pepper, and celery to the skillet. Cook, stirring occasionally, until the vegetables are softened, about 5-7 minutes.
3. Stir in the minced garlic and cook for another minute until fragrant.
4. Add the fresh corn kernels to the skillet. Cook, stirring occasionally, for 5-7 minutes, until the corn is tender and slightly caramelized.
5. Stir in the Cajun seasoning, paprika, cayenne pepper, salt, and black pepper to taste.
6. Pour in the chicken or vegetable broth, stirring to scrape up any browned bits from the bottom of the skillet. Let the mixture simmer for a few minutes to allow the flavors to meld together.
7. Once the liquid has reduced and thickened slightly, stir in the cooked bacon pieces.
8. Taste and adjust the seasoning of the Maque Choux if needed.

9. Serve the Cajun Corn Maque Choux hot, garnished with chopped fresh parsley.
10. Enjoy your flavorful and comforting Cajun Corn Maque Choux as a delicious side dish or light main course!

Stuffed Bell Peppers (Cajun Style)

Ingredients:

- 4 large bell peppers (any color), tops removed and seeds removed
- 1 tablespoon vegetable oil
- 1 onion, diced
- 2 cloves garlic, minced
- 1 stalk celery, diced
- 1 bell pepper (any color), diced
- 1 lb (about 450g) ground beef or turkey
- 1 cup cooked rice
- 1 can (14.5 oz) diced tomatoes, drained
- 1 tablespoon Cajun seasoning
- 1/2 teaspoon paprika
- Salt and black pepper to taste
- 1 cup shredded cheddar cheese
- Chopped fresh parsley for garnish (optional)

Instructions:

1. Preheat your oven to 375°F (190°C).
2. In a large skillet, heat the vegetable oil over medium heat. Add the diced onion, minced garlic, diced celery, and diced bell pepper. Cook, stirring occasionally, until the vegetables are softened, about 5-7 minutes.
3. Add the ground beef or turkey to the skillet. Cook, breaking up the meat with a spoon, until browned and cooked through, about 5-7 minutes.
4. Stir in the cooked rice, diced tomatoes, Cajun seasoning, paprika, salt, and black pepper. Cook for another 2-3 minutes to allow the flavors to meld together.
5. Remove the skillet from the heat and let the mixture cool slightly.
6. Stuff each bell pepper with the meat and rice mixture, pressing it down gently to pack it in.
7. Place the stuffed bell peppers in a baking dish or on a baking sheet lined with parchment paper.
8. Cover the baking dish with aluminum foil and bake in the preheated oven for 25-30 minutes.
9. Remove the foil from the baking dish and sprinkle the shredded cheddar cheese over the tops of the stuffed bell peppers.
10. Return the baking dish to the oven and bake, uncovered, for another 10-15 minutes, or until the cheese is melted and bubbly.
11. Remove the stuffed bell peppers from the oven and let them cool for a few minutes before serving.

12. Garnish the stuffed bell peppers with chopped fresh parsley, if desired, before serving.
13. Enjoy your flavorful and satisfying Cajun-style stuffed bell peppers as a delicious main course!

Cajun Red Beans and Rice

Ingredients:

- 1 lb (about 450g) dried red kidney beans
- 1 tablespoon vegetable oil
- 1 onion, diced
- 1 bell pepper, diced
- 2 celery stalks, diced
- 3 cloves garlic, minced
- 1 lb (about 450g) smoked sausage, such as andouille, sliced
- 1 ham hock or 1 cup diced ham (optional, for extra flavor)
- 6 cups chicken or vegetable broth
- 2 bay leaves
- 1 tablespoon Cajun seasoning
- 1 teaspoon dried thyme
- 1/2 teaspoon paprika
- 1/4 teaspoon cayenne pepper (adjust to taste)
- Salt and black pepper to taste
- Cooked white rice, for serving
- Chopped green onions (scallions) for garnish

Instructions:

1. Rinse the dried red kidney beans under cold water and remove any debris or stones. Place the beans in a large bowl and cover with water. Let them soak overnight, or use the quick soak method by bringing them to a boil, then removing from heat and letting them soak for 1 hour.
2. In a large Dutch oven or heavy-bottomed pot, heat the vegetable oil over medium heat. Add the diced onion, bell pepper, and celery. Cook, stirring occasionally, until the vegetables are softened, about 5-7 minutes.
3. Add the minced garlic to the pot and cook for another minute until fragrant.
4. Add the sliced smoked sausage to the pot. Cook, stirring occasionally, until the sausage is lightly browned, about 5 minutes.
5. Drain the soaked red kidney beans and add them to the pot. Stir to combine with the vegetables and sausage.

6. Add the chicken or vegetable broth to the pot, along with the ham hock or diced ham (if using), bay leaves, Cajun seasoning, dried thyme, paprika, cayenne pepper, salt, and black pepper.
7. Bring the mixture to a boil, then reduce the heat to low. Cover and let it simmer for 1.5 to 2 hours, stirring occasionally, until the beans are tender and the sauce has thickened. If the sauce becomes too thick, you can add more broth or water as needed.
8. Taste and adjust the seasoning of the red beans and rice if needed.
9. Remove the bay leaves and ham hock (if using) from the pot before serving.
10. Serve the Cajun red beans and rice hot over cooked white rice.
11. Garnish with chopped green onions (scallions) before serving.
12. Enjoy your delicious and comforting Cajun red beans and rice!

Cajun Chicken and Sausage Jambalaya

Ingredients:

- 1 lb (about 450g) boneless, skinless chicken thighs, cut into bite-sized pieces
- 1 lb (about 450g) andouille sausage, sliced
- 1 onion, diced
- 1 bell pepper, diced
- 2 celery stalks, diced
- 3 cloves garlic, minced
- 1 can (14.5 oz) diced tomatoes
- 2 cups long-grain white rice
- 4 cups chicken broth
- 2 bay leaves
- 1 tablespoon Cajun seasoning
- 1/2 teaspoon dried thyme
- 1/2 teaspoon dried oregano
- 1/4 teaspoon cayenne pepper (adjust to taste)
- Salt and black pepper to taste
- Chopped fresh parsley for garnish
- Chopped green onions (scallions) for garnish

Instructions:

1. In a large Dutch oven or heavy-bottomed pot, heat some oil over medium-high heat. Add the chicken pieces and cook until browned on all sides, about 5-7 minutes. Remove the chicken from the pot and set aside.
2. In the same pot, add the sliced andouille sausage. Cook until browned, about 5 minutes. Remove the sausage from the pot and set aside.
3. Add a bit more oil to the pot if needed. Add the diced onion, bell pepper, and celery. Cook, stirring occasionally, until the vegetables are softened, about 5-7 minutes.
4. Add the minced garlic to the pot and cook for another minute until fragrant.
5. Stir in the diced tomatoes (with their juices) and cook for 2-3 minutes.
6. Return the chicken and sausage to the pot. Add the rice, chicken broth, bay leaves, Cajun seasoning, dried thyme, dried oregano, cayenne pepper, salt, and black pepper. Stir to combine.

7. Bring the mixture to a boil, then reduce the heat to low. Cover and let it simmer for about 20-25 minutes, or until the rice is cooked and the liquid is absorbed.
8. Once the rice is cooked, remove the pot from the heat. Let the jambalaya sit, covered, for a few minutes to allow the flavors to meld together.
9. Remove the bay leaves from the pot before serving.
10. Serve the Cajun chicken and sausage jambalaya hot, garnished with chopped fresh parsley and chopped green onions.
11. Enjoy your delicious and flavorful Cajun jambalaya!

Cajun Boudin Balls

Ingredients:

- 1 lb (about 450g) Cajun-style boudin sausage
- 1 cup all-purpose flour
- 2 large eggs, beaten
- 1 cup seasoned breadcrumbs or cornmeal
- Vegetable oil, for frying
- Cajun seasoning, for seasoning (optional)
- Dipping sauce of your choice (such as hot sauce, mustard, or remoulade sauce)

Instructions:

1. Remove the boudin sausage from its casing and place it in a mixing bowl. Use a fork to break up the sausage and mix it well.
2. Shape the boudin mixture into small balls, about 1-2 inches in diameter. Place the balls on a baking sheet lined with parchment paper.
3. In three separate shallow bowls, place the all-purpose flour, beaten eggs, and seasoned breadcrumbs or cornmeal.
4. Roll each boudin ball in the flour until coated, then dip it into the beaten eggs, and finally roll it in the seasoned breadcrumbs or cornmeal until evenly coated. Place the coated balls back on the baking sheet.
5. Heat vegetable oil in a deep fryer or large skillet to 350°F (175°C).
6. Carefully add the boudin balls to the hot oil in batches, making sure not to overcrowd the pan. Fry the balls for 3-4 minutes, or until they are golden brown and crispy on the outside.
7. Use a slotted spoon to remove the fried boudin balls from the oil and transfer them to a plate lined with paper towels to drain excess oil.
8. While still hot, sprinkle the fried boudin balls with Cajun seasoning for extra flavor, if desired.
9. Serve the Cajun boudin balls hot, with your choice of dipping sauce on the side.
10. Enjoy your delicious and flavorful Cajun boudin balls as a tasty appetizer or snack!

Cajun Dirty Rice

Ingredients:

- 1 cup long-grain white rice
- 1 lb (about 450g) ground pork or ground beef
- 1 onion, finely chopped
- 1 bell pepper, finely chopped
- 2 celery stalks, finely chopped
- 3 cloves garlic, minced
- 4 slices bacon, chopped
- 2 cups chicken or beef broth
- 2 tablespoons vegetable oil
- 2 tablespoons Cajun seasoning
- 1 teaspoon dried thyme
- 1 teaspoon dried oregano
- 1/2 teaspoon paprika
- 1/4 teaspoon cayenne pepper (adjust to taste)
- Salt and black pepper to taste
- Chopped green onions (scallions) for garnish

Instructions:

1. Rinse the rice under cold water until the water runs clear. Drain well and set aside.
2. In a large skillet or sauté pan, cook the chopped bacon over medium heat until crisp. Remove the bacon from the pan and set aside, leaving the bacon grease in the pan.
3. Add the vegetable oil to the skillet with the bacon grease. Add the chopped onion, bell pepper, and celery. Cook, stirring occasionally, until the vegetables are softened, about 5-7 minutes.
4. Add the minced garlic to the skillet and cook for another minute until fragrant.
5. Add the ground pork or beef to the skillet. Cook, breaking up the meat with a spoon, until browned and cooked through, about 5-7 minutes.
6. Stir in the Cajun seasoning, dried thyme, dried oregano, paprika, cayenne pepper, salt, and black pepper to taste.
7. Add the rinsed and drained rice to the skillet. Cook, stirring constantly, for 1-2 minutes to toast the rice slightly and coat it with the spices.
8. Pour in the chicken or beef broth, stirring to combine and scrape up any browned bits from the bottom of the skillet.
9. Bring the mixture to a boil, then reduce the heat to low. Cover and let it simmer for about 15-20 minutes, or until the rice is cooked and the liquid is absorbed.
10. Once the rice is cooked, remove the skillet from the heat. Fluff the rice with a fork and stir in the cooked bacon pieces.

11. Taste and adjust the seasoning of the dirty rice if needed.
12. Serve the Cajun dirty rice hot, garnished with chopped green onions (scallions) for extra flavor.
13. Enjoy your flavorful and comforting Cajun dirty rice as a delicious side dish or light main course!

Cajun Blackened Catfish

Ingredients:

- 4 catfish fillets, about 6-8 ounces each
- 2 tablespoons Cajun seasoning
- 1 teaspoon paprika
- 1/2 teaspoon garlic powder
- 1/2 teaspoon onion powder
- 1/2 teaspoon dried thyme
- 1/2 teaspoon dried oregano
- 1/4 teaspoon cayenne pepper (adjust to taste)
- Salt to taste
- 2 tablespoons unsalted butter, melted
- Vegetable oil or clarified butter, for searing
- Lemon wedges, for serving
- Chopped fresh parsley for garnish (optional)

Instructions:

1. In a small bowl, combine the Cajun seasoning, paprika, garlic powder, onion powder, dried thyme, dried oregano, cayenne pepper, and salt.
2. Pat the catfish fillets dry with paper towels. Brush both sides of each fillet with melted butter.
3. Sprinkle the Cajun seasoning mixture evenly over both sides of each catfish fillet, pressing gently to adhere.
4. Heat a cast iron skillet or heavy-bottomed pan over high heat until it is smoking hot.
5. Add enough vegetable oil or clarified butter to the skillet to coat the bottom. Carefully place the seasoned catfish fillets in the skillet.
6. Cook the catfish fillets for 2-3 minutes on each side, or until they are blackened and crispy on the outside and cooked through on the inside. The cooking time will depend on the thickness of the fillets.
7. Remove the blackened catfish fillets from the skillet and transfer them to a serving platter.
8. Serve the Cajun blackened catfish hot, garnished with lemon wedges and chopped fresh parsley if desired.
9. Enjoy your delicious and flavorful Cajun blackened catfish as a main course, served with your favorite sides such as rice, vegetables, or a fresh salad!

Shrimp Po' Boy with Remoulade Sauce

Ingredients:

For the Shrimp:

- 1 lb (about 450g) large shrimp, peeled and deveined
- 1 cup all-purpose flour
- 1 teaspoon Cajun seasoning
- 1/2 teaspoon paprika
- 1/4 teaspoon cayenne pepper (adjust to taste)
- Salt and black pepper to taste
- Vegetable oil, for frying

For the Remoulade Sauce:

- 1/2 cup mayonnaise
- 2 tablespoons Dijon mustard
- 1 tablespoon prepared horseradish
- 1 tablespoon chopped fresh parsley
- 1 tablespoon chopped green onions (scallions)
- 1 tablespoon chopped celery
- 1 tablespoon chopped dill pickles or pickle relish
- 1 clove garlic, minced
- 1 teaspoon hot sauce (adjust to taste)
- 1 teaspoon Worcestershire sauce
- Salt and black pepper to taste

For Serving:

- French bread rolls (po' boy rolls)
- Shredded lettuce
- Sliced tomatoes
- Sliced pickles

Instructions:

1. To make the remoulade sauce, in a small bowl, combine the mayonnaise, Dijon mustard, prepared horseradish, chopped parsley, chopped green onions, chopped celery, chopped dill pickles or pickle relish, minced garlic, hot sauce, Worcestershire sauce, salt, and black pepper. Mix well to combine. Cover and refrigerate until ready to use.
2. In a shallow dish, combine the all-purpose flour, Cajun seasoning, paprika, cayenne pepper, salt, and black pepper. Mix well.
3. Pat the peeled and deveined shrimp dry with paper towels.
4. Heat vegetable oil in a large skillet or deep fryer to 350°F (175°C).
5. Dredge the shrimp in the seasoned flour mixture, shaking off any excess.
6. Carefully add the shrimp to the hot oil in batches, making sure not to overcrowd the pan. Fry the shrimp for 2-3 minutes, or until they are golden brown and crispy. Remove the fried shrimp from the oil and drain on paper towels. Repeat with the remaining shrimp.
7. Slice the French bread rolls in half horizontally.
8. Spread a generous amount of remoulade sauce on the bottom half of each roll.
9. Arrange a layer of shredded lettuce, sliced tomatoes, and sliced pickles on top of the remoulade sauce.
10. Place the fried shrimp on top of the vegetables.
11. Close the sandwiches with the top halves of the French bread rolls.
12. Serve the shrimp po' boy sandwiches immediately, with extra remoulade sauce on the side for dipping.
13. Enjoy your delicious and flavorful shrimp po' boy sandwiches!

Cajun Crab Cakes with Creole Mustard Sauce

Ingredients:

For the Crab Cakes:

- 1 lb (about 450g) lump crabmeat, drained
- 1/2 cup breadcrumbs
- 1/4 cup mayonnaise
- 1 large egg, lightly beaten
- 2 tablespoons chopped green onions (scallions)
- 2 tablespoons chopped fresh parsley
- 1 tablespoon Cajun seasoning
- 1 teaspoon Dijon mustard
- 1/2 teaspoon Worcestershire sauce
- Salt and black pepper to taste
- Vegetable oil, for frying

For the Creole Mustard Sauce:

- 1/2 cup mayonnaise
- 2 tablespoons Creole mustard (or substitute with Dijon mustard)
- 1 tablespoon lemon juice
- 1 tablespoon chopped fresh parsley
- 1 teaspoon hot sauce (adjust to taste)
- Salt and black pepper to taste

Instructions:

1. In a large mixing bowl, combine the lump crabmeat, breadcrumbs, mayonnaise, beaten egg, chopped green onions, chopped fresh parsley, Cajun seasoning, Dijon mustard, Worcestershire sauce, salt, and black pepper. Gently mix until well combined.
2. Divide the crab mixture into equal portions and shape each portion into a patty. Place the crab cakes on a baking sheet lined with parchment paper. Cover and refrigerate for at least 30 minutes to firm up.
3. While the crab cakes are chilling, prepare the Creole mustard sauce. In a small bowl, combine the mayonnaise, Creole mustard, lemon juice, chopped parsley, hot sauce, salt, and black pepper. Mix well. Cover and refrigerate until ready to serve.
4. Heat vegetable oil in a large skillet over medium-high heat.

5. Carefully place the chilled crab cakes in the hot skillet. Cook for 3-4 minutes on each side, or until golden brown and heated through. You may need to work in batches depending on the size of your skillet.
6. Once the crab cakes are cooked, remove them from the skillet and drain on paper towels to remove excess oil.
7. Serve the Cajun crab cakes hot, with the Creole mustard sauce on the side for dipping.
8. Garnish with additional chopped parsley or lemon wedges if desired.
9. Enjoy your delicious Cajun crab cakes with tangy Creole mustard sauce as an appetizer or main course!

Cajun Shrimp and Andouille Sausage Pasta

Ingredients:

- 8 oz (about 225g) penne or fettuccine pasta
- 1 lb (about 450g) large shrimp, peeled and deveined
- 1/2 lb (about 225g) andouille sausage, sliced
- 1 tablespoon Cajun seasoning
- 1 tablespoon olive oil
- 2 tablespoons unsalted butter
- 1 onion, diced
- 1 bell pepper, diced
- 2 cloves garlic, minced
- 1 cup chicken broth
- 1 cup heavy cream
- 1/4 cup grated Parmesan cheese
- Salt and black pepper to taste
- Chopped fresh parsley for garnish (optional)

Instructions:

1. Cook the pasta according to the package instructions until al dente. Drain and set aside.
2. In a large skillet or sauté pan, heat the olive oil over medium-high heat. Add the sliced andouille sausage and cook until browned, about 5 minutes. Remove the sausage from the skillet and set aside.
3. In the same skillet, add the shrimp and sprinkle with Cajun seasoning. Cook for 2-3 minutes on each side, until pink and cooked through. Remove the shrimp from the skillet and set aside.
4. In the same skillet, melt the butter over medium heat. Add the diced onion and bell pepper. Cook, stirring occasionally, until the vegetables are softened, about 5 minutes. Add the minced garlic and cook for another minute until fragrant.
5. Pour the chicken broth into the skillet, scraping up any browned bits from the bottom of the pan. Let the broth simmer for a few minutes to reduce slightly.
6. Stir in the heavy cream and grated Parmesan cheese. Let the sauce simmer for 2-3 minutes, until it thickens slightly.
7. Return the cooked pasta, andouille sausage, and shrimp to the skillet. Toss everything together until evenly coated in the sauce. Season with salt and black pepper to taste.
8. Garnish the Cajun shrimp and andouille sausage pasta with chopped fresh parsley, if desired.
9. Serve hot and enjoy your flavorful and creamy Cajun pasta dish!

Feel free to adjust the Cajun seasoning and spice level to suit your taste preferences.

Cajun Shrimp and Crab Salad

Ingredients:

For the Salad:

- 1 lb (about 450g) large shrimp, peeled and deveined
- 1 lb (about 450g) lump crabmeat, drained
- 4 cups mixed salad greens (such as lettuce, spinach, and arugula)
- 1 bell pepper, thinly sliced
- 1 cucumber, thinly sliced
- 1 pint cherry tomatoes, halved
- 1/4 cup chopped fresh parsley
- Lemon wedges, for serving

For the Cajun Dressing:

- 1/4 cup mayonnaise
- 2 tablespoons Creole mustard (or substitute with Dijon mustard)
- 1 tablespoon apple cider vinegar
- 1 tablespoon lemon juice
- 1 tablespoon chopped fresh parsley
- 1 teaspoon Cajun seasoning
- 1/2 teaspoon paprika
- 1/4 teaspoon cayenne pepper (adjust to taste)
- Salt and black pepper to taste

Instructions:

1. In a large pot of boiling salted water, cook the shrimp for 2-3 minutes, or until pink and cooked through. Drain the shrimp and rinse with cold water to stop the cooking process. Set aside.
2. In a small bowl, whisk together all the ingredients for the Cajun dressing until well combined. Taste and adjust the seasoning as needed. Set aside.
3. In a large mixing bowl, combine the cooked shrimp, lump crabmeat, mixed salad greens, sliced bell pepper, sliced cucumber, halved cherry tomatoes, and chopped fresh parsley.
4. Drizzle the Cajun dressing over the salad and toss gently to coat everything evenly.
5. Divide the Cajun shrimp and crab salad among serving plates or bowls.
6. Serve immediately, garnished with lemon wedges on the side for squeezing over the salad.

7. Enjoy your delicious and flavorful Cajun shrimp and crab salad as a refreshing appetizer or light meal!

Feel free to customize the salad by adding other vegetables or toppings of your choice, such as avocado, red onion, or croutons. Adjust the spice level of the Cajun dressing to suit your taste preferences.

Cajun Chicken and Sausage Gumbo

Ingredients:

For the Gumbo:

- 1/2 cup vegetable oil
- 1/2 cup all-purpose flour (for making roux)
- 1 onion, diced
- 1 bell pepper, diced
- 2 celery stalks, diced
- 3 cloves garlic, minced
- 1 lb (about 450g) boneless, skinless chicken thighs, cut into bite-sized pieces
- 1/2 lb (about 225g) andouille sausage, sliced
- 8 cups chicken broth
- 2 bay leaves
- 1 teaspoon dried thyme
- 1 teaspoon dried oregano
- 1 teaspoon Cajun seasoning
- Salt and black pepper to taste
- Cooked white rice, for serving
- Chopped green onions (scallions) for garnish
- File powder (optional, for thickening)

Instructions:

1. In a large Dutch oven or heavy-bottomed pot, heat the vegetable oil over medium heat. Gradually whisk in the all-purpose flour to make a roux. Cook the roux, stirring constantly, until it turns a dark caramel color, about 20-30 minutes. Be careful not to burn the roux.
2. Add the diced onion, bell pepper, celery, and minced garlic to the pot. Cook, stirring occasionally, until the vegetables are softened, about 5-7 minutes.
3. Add the bite-sized pieces of chicken thighs and sliced andouille sausage to the pot. Cook, stirring occasionally, until the chicken is browned on all sides, about 5 minutes.
4. Pour in the chicken broth, stirring to scrape up any browned bits from the bottom of the pot. Add the bay leaves, dried thyme, dried oregano, Cajun seasoning, salt, and black pepper to taste.
5. Bring the gumbo to a boil, then reduce the heat to low. Let it simmer, uncovered, for about 1-1.5 hours, stirring occasionally, until the flavors meld together and the gumbo thickens slightly. If desired, you can add file powder during the last 15 minutes of cooking to further thicken the gumbo.

6. Taste and adjust the seasoning of the gumbo if needed.
7. Remove the bay leaves from the gumbo before serving.
8. Serve the Cajun chicken and sausage gumbo hot over cooked white rice.
9. Garnish with chopped green onions (scallions) before serving.
10. Enjoy your flavorful and comforting Cajun gumbo as a delicious main course!

Cajun Shrimp and Sausage Jambalaya

Ingredients:

For the Gumbo:

- 1/2 cup vegetable oil
- 1/2 cup all-purpose flour (for making roux)
- 1 onion, diced
- 1 bell pepper, diced
- 2 celery stalks, diced
- 3 cloves garlic, minced
- 1 lb (about 450g) boneless, skinless chicken thighs, cut into bite-sized pieces
- 1/2 lb (about 225g) andouille sausage, sliced
- 8 cups chicken broth
- 2 bay leaves
- 1 teaspoon dried thyme
- 1 teaspoon dried oregano
- 1 teaspoon Cajun seasoning
- Salt and black pepper to taste
- Cooked white rice, for serving
- Chopped green onions (scallions) for garnish
- File powder (optional, for thickening)

Instructions:

1. In a large Dutch oven or heavy-bottomed pot, heat the vegetable oil over medium heat. Gradually whisk in the all-purpose flour to make a roux. Cook the roux, stirring constantly, until it turns a dark caramel color, about 20-30 minutes. Be careful not to burn the roux.
2. Add the diced onion, bell pepper, celery, and minced garlic to the pot. Cook, stirring occasionally, until the vegetables are softened, about 5-7 minutes.
3. Add the bite-sized pieces of chicken thighs and sliced andouille sausage to the pot. Cook, stirring occasionally, until the chicken is browned on all sides, about 5 minutes.
4. Pour in the chicken broth, stirring to scrape up any browned bits from the bottom of the pot. Add the bay leaves, dried thyme, dried oregano, Cajun seasoning, salt, and black pepper to taste.
5. Bring the gumbo to a boil, then reduce the heat to low. Let it simmer, uncovered, for about 1-1.5 hours, stirring occasionally, until the flavors meld together and the gumbo thickens slightly. If desired, you can add file powder during the last 15 minutes of cooking to further thicken the gumbo.

6. Taste and adjust the seasoning of the gumbo if needed.
7. Remove the bay leaves from the gumbo before serving.
8. Serve the Cajun chicken and sausage gumbo hot over cooked white rice.
9. Garnish with chopped green onions (scallions) before serving.
10. Enjoy your flavorful and comforting Cajun gumbo as a delicious main course!

www.ingramcontent.com/pod-product-compliance
Lightning Source LLC
LaVergne TN
LVHW062048070526
838201LV00080B/2199